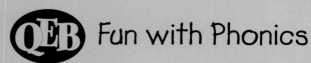

QEB Fun with Phonics

Meeble's Magic Box

Learn ch, sh and th words with Meeble

Copyright © QEB Publishing, Inc. 2006

First published in the United States in 2006 by
QEB Publishing, Inc.
23062 La Cadena Drive
Laguna Hills, CA 92653
www.qeb-publishing.com

Library of Congress Control Number:
2005911017

ISBN 9-781-59566-221-7

Written by Wendy Body
Designed by Alix Wood
Editor Gina Nuttall
Illustrations Caroline Martin

Publisher Steve Evans
Editorial Director Jean Coppendale
Art Director Zeta Davies

Printed and bound in China

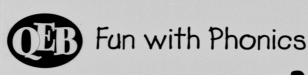

QEB Fun with Phonics

Meeble's Magic Box

Learn ch, sh, and th words with Meeble

Wendy Body

What's in Meeble's magic box today?

What's in Meeble's magic box today?

What's in Meeble's magic box today?

What's in Meeble's magic box today?

What's in Meeble's magic box today?

What's in Meeble's magic box today?

What's in Meeble's magic box today?

What's in Meeble's magic box today?

What's in Meeble's magic box today?

A **sh**y little **sh**ark!

21

What's in Meeble's magic box today?

23

Parents' and teachers' notes

• Before reading the book, read the title and look at the front cover illustration with your child. Talk about what the character is (a monster), what his name is (Meeble) and what Meeble is doing. Can your child think of anyone he or she knows with a name beginning with the same letter as Meeble?

• As you read the book to your child, run your finger along underneath the text. This will help your child to follow the reading and focus on how the words both look and sound.

• On the first or second rereading, leave out some of the words being used to illustrate the letter sounds and let your child say them. Point to the illustration to help your child supply the word.

• Draw your child's attention to the beginning of words—e.g. "This word begins with an **n** (letter name) and it makes a **nnnnnn** sound." or "This word begins with **s** (letter name) and an **h**. When we put them together, they make a **shhh** sound."

• When you are talking about letter sounds, try not to add too much of an **uh** sound. Say **mmm** instead of **muh**, **ssss** instead of **suh**. Saying letter sounds as carefully as possible helps children when they are trying to build up or spell words: **ber-u-ter** doesn't sound much like **but**!

• Talk about and discuss the characters on each page—what they look like, what they are doing and why, and what they might be thinking.

• Encourage your child to express opinions and preferences—e.g. "Which picture do you like the most?" "Which part of the book did you like the best? Why?"

• Choose any page and use the illustration to play "I Spy" using letter sounds rather than names.

• Make a set of three cards, one each with **ch**, **sh**, and **th** on it. Give your child a card and ask him or her to match the card to words in the book that begin with those letters. Encourage your child to say each word he or she finds. Can they think of other words beginning with those sounds?

• On a piece of paper, write "[Your child's name]'s Magic Box." Draw three boxes on a piece of paper. Label each one with **ch**, **sh**, or **th**. Ask your child to think of words beginning with these sounds and write them in the appropriate box.

• Talk about words: their meaning, how they sound, how they look, and how they are spelled. However, if your child gets restless or bored, stop. Enjoyment of the book or activity is essential if we want children to grow up valuing books and reading!